The COMPLETE BULLSHIT-FREE and TOTALLY TESTED WRITING GUIDE

HOW TO MAKE PUBLISHERS, AGENTS, EDITORS & READERS FALL IN LOVE WITH YOUR WORK

GABE BERMAN

Published by:
5-12 Media
East Rockaway, New York

ISBN: 978-0-6157948-0-8

Copyright © 2013 by Gabe Berman

All rights reserved. No part of this publication may be reproduced, scanned, uploaded, stored in a retrieval system, or transmitted, in any form or by any means, electronic, mechanical, photocopying, recording, or otherwise, without the prior written permission of the publisher.

Cover and Interior Design:
Gary A. Rosenberg • www.thebookcouple.com

Printed in the United States of America

Dedicated to the one
who never doubted me:

me

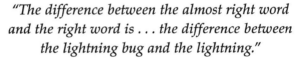

"The difference between the almost right word and the right word is . . . the difference between the lightning bug and the lightning."

—MARK TWAIN

Get comfortable because I want to tell you something.

Ready?

You're extraordinary.

Yes, I have the right person. You. The person reading these words right now: you're extraordinary.

Regardless of how you may feel in this moment and regardless of what you may have heard in the past, you are in fact extraordinary.

How do I know?

Because you're a writer. And writers, the ones who write from the gut, are absolutely extraordinary.

But why should you listen to what I have to say?

That's a valid question.

I'm obviously not Mark Twain or Ernest Hemingway.

I'm just Gabe Berman. I was just another ordinary person on this planet of ours.

But like you, I chose to be extraordinary. The butterfly flapped its wings. The universe was set into motion. I wrote for the *Miami Herald* for eight years. My book, *Live Like a Fruit Fly—The Secret You Already Know,* was endorsed by Deepak Chopra.

Was it luck or am I that talented?

Yes.

(By the way, you just read the introduction. I didn't call it the introduction because if you're anything like me, you would have just skipped right over it.)

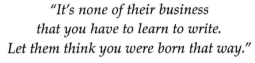

*"It's none of their business
that you have to learn to write.
Let them think you were born that way."*

—ERNEST HEMINGWAY

CHAPTER 1

Unless you're a celebrity, no one gives a shit about you.

I'm sorry, but not only is that the absolute truth, it's the second most critical piece of writing advice I can pass along.

No one gives a shit about you. Let's allow that to marinate a bit.

You know what, why don't you get up and take a walk around the block, and I'll meet you at the beginning of the next chapter in a little while.

CHAPTER 2

Okay good, you're back. After receiving the news in the last chapter, I'm sure many people have already chucked this book onto the compost pile.

I'm happy you didn't and your destiny is as well.

Before we move forward, let's take a moment to review: you're extraordinary but no one gives a shit about you.

How many times am I going to remind you that no one gives a shit about you?

Until it permeates your psyche, flows through your veins and permanently entangles with your DNA.

I wouldn't go as far as getting it tattooed on your forearm in 18-pt Times New Roman (or even in an understated Helvetica), but it might not be a bad idea to put a sign near your desk that clearly reads: NO ONE GIVES A SHIT ABOUT YOU.

If you doubt this at all, if you actually think for a minute that a few potential readers out there might give a shit about you, then you need to get that sign made in flashing neon.

Those seven words, coupled with your raw talent and the number one most critical writing rule (which we'll get to), will lead you to mastery.

And trust me, I know those seven words sting. But I'd rather you hear them from me now than from your loved ones down the road.

They're not going to come out of nowhere one day and blindside you with a phone call that sounds something like, "Hey, what's up? Nothing much here. Just saw the new Batman. It was pretty good. Oh, by the way, I don't give a shit about you."

They're going to tell you in between the lines. In response to an email you sent.

Your email will say:

Hi :)

When you have time, can you please check out this new thing I wrote? Please just be honest with me and PLEASE don't show it to anyone else.

And if you don't remember that no one gives a shit about you as you wrote your new piece, your friends and family will respond with:

You have such a great imagination!

or

I didn't know you knew so much about horses!

or

That's such a sad story. I'm happy you didn't give up!

or

You have such a great imagination. I didn't know you knew so much about horses. I'm so happy you didn't give up, and I heard Starbucks is hiring.

In other words: I don't give a shit about you.

But if you remember those seven words as you write, you'll get responses similar to:

I loved what I perceive to be the author's authenticity—both his strength and his vulnerability transmitted through the stories of his own life.

and

It's like sitting on the couch with your best friend and talking until the sun comes up.

and

After I read this book, I purchased three more as gifts—a MUST read! Great insight into finding happiness in this beautiful, yet sometimes baffling, world of ours. The author

> *has accomplished sharing personal life experiences in both a humorous and prolific style—looking forward to more of his "words of wisdom"!*

and

> *I feel like enlarging the pages and wallpapering my house with them. That's how big his message is. Brilliant.*

I just copy/pasted these reviews from amazon.com. I'm grateful to say, they're reviews of my book. Just four of the ninety-three 5-star reviews.

Yes, I'm a decently talented writer. Yes, my book contains life-changing and life-affirming messages. But as you and I know, we're FAR from alone in the decently talented writer department. The ONLY reason my messages resonate as well as they do is because of the flashing green and orange neon sign in my brain that reads: NO ONE GIVES A SHIT ABOUT YOU.

But here's the beautiful irony: being aware that no one gives a shit about me caused readers to really give a shit about me. And to reiterate, I realize I'm not even in the same neighborhood as heavyweights like Salinger and Vonnegut, but even if you hate history, I can write 1,000 words about the Spanish-American War and by the end of the piece, you'll feel as though you and I are old friends.

How do I know no one gives a shit about me? Because the truth is, I don't give a shit about them.

Wait. Please put down the phone. Before you call Deepak Chopra to tell him I'm a big phony, just hear me out for a minute.

I care deeply about people and I know you're deeply cared about. When I say *unless you're a celebrity, no one gives a shit about you,* it's because readers only give a shit about themselves. And you know what, can you blame them?

Life is short. If you're expecting us to trade our precious time for an opportunity to read your words, it better be an even swap. But if you really care what people think, and you should if you want to get published, you'll want us to feel like we made out like bandits in the deal. You'll want to make us feel that we couldn't imagine spending our time in any other way. To the point we'll say, "I feel like enlarging the pages and wallpapering my house with them."

How do you accomplish this? YOU PUT YOURSELF IN THE READER'S SHOES.

As fellow humans, we naturally care if your mom was sick and you visited her in the hospital, but unless you're Bruce Springsteen, not for more than two sentences. And that might even be stretching it.

The Boss can write pages about buying gum in the gift shop and I'll hang on every word. Since you and I are nobodies, we don't have that luxury. EVERY WORD WE WRITE AND EVERY SPACE BETWEEN THOSE WORDS MUST MEAN SOMETHING TO THE READER!

If you dare describe the hospital room in vivid detail, just to show off your talent for description, I'm throwing your book in the garbage. I won't even try to resell it. Right in the goddamn garbage it goes.

I don't give a shit how talented you are. I don't care that you can paint a canvas with your words. If I can't connect with it, it means nothing to me. But I will literally love you forever and buy everything you write if your words find their way into my heart. And it wouldn't matter if you only used the vocabulary of an eight-year-old and your book was written on toilet paper with crayons. Stick to my soul and I'm yours.

This is the biggest mistake writers make, professionals and novices alike. The ability to write well doesn't necessarily mean that people are going to give a shit enough to make it through the first page.

Remember the reader.

Your mom is in the hospital? Give me a reason to connect with it and do so right away. You write about horses or space battles? Or horses *in* space battles? Perfect. I love it. Just make me feel what you feel.

You had your heart broken? Welcome to the club. So don't talk to me as if I can't imagine what you've been through. You insult my own experiences if you do. Rather, talk to me as if you know I've been down a similar path. Put us on the same page. I'll be your friend. I'll wallpaper my walls with your words.

And for the love of all things holy, don't even think about setting the scene of September 11th for me. As if I haven't thought about it every day since. You can safely assume we all know what happened. But if I get that you get it, we'll be brothers in arms from this day forward.

There's a fine line between writing too much and too little but it's worth dedicating your entire career to perfecting it. It doesn't matter if you ever do. It just matters that you keep getting closer.

"In writing . . . remember that the biggest stories are not written about wars, or about politics, or even murders. The biggest stories are written about the things which draw human beings closer together."

—SUSAN GLASPELL, *LITTLE MASKS*

CHAPTER 3

I have a confession to make.

Months have passed since the last chapter. Just when you're on a roll, Life sometimes gets in the way.

But unless I fessed up, you, the reader, wouldn't have had the foggiest. You're just sitting there right now, maybe in your pajamas, and all you had to do is turn the page to discover the intriguing sentence, "I have a confession to make."

Even if you hate me, despise this book, and have a vendetta against the entirety of Earth's written languages, it's physically impossible to read a sentence like, "I have a confession to make," and not immediately point your eyeballs to the next sentence.

Right?

Hold on a second. . . . *and not immediately point* . . . Is that grammatically correct?

Honestly, I have no idea. But who cares? I write like I talk and that creates the flow.

If I worried about grammar all of the time, it would sound like I'm worrying about grammar all of the time and you'd end up saying to yourself, "You know what, I don't give a shit about you."

I'm sure it breaks a nitpicky rule of writing but as my dad said—stupid rules are made to be broken (see, I just made up the word "nitpicky" and there's nothing my high school English teachers can do about it).

Getting back to where we were, do you see how perfectly it all worked out?

If I forced myself to write this chapter right after I finished the last one, "I must make a confession," wouldn't have had a reason to tunnel its way into my consciousness while I was rinsing the shampoo out of my hair today.

And if that hadn't happened, I wouldn't have made it here with you. Where's here? Exactly where we need to be.

Because now I'm ready to make two points. Two points I knew I needed to make but, until now, were unintelligible ideas rolling around in the dark corners of my mind like haphazard tumbleweeds.

The question is: would I have been able to make these points earlier? Of course. But another question must now be asked: would it have unfolded as beautifully organic? No way in hell.

On some level deep down in your DNA, you'd know I'd be forcing the puzzle pieces together. And eventually you'd be like, "I just don't give a shit about this guy," and you'd end up ignoring, rightfully so, any writing advice I spewed out for you.

And now, without further ado, the two points:

ONE: reading is like cooking. It can take hours to prepare, and then the meal is over in minutes. Good, that means you've done your job well.

Your guests will never be able to comprehend the love and energy it takes to "whip up" a perfect feast but they wouldn't have cleaned their plates with such passion if you rushed or forced the process.

Don't rush or force the process. Ever.

Life is short and there's plenty to do, but I'd rather write ten words that will stir the souls of mankind than ten thousand that will never get past the flesh.

TWO: writers write. And some say you should write every day.

They're probably correct. I'm sure my phrasing would become more graceful. But if you're writing with the intention of being read, and don't kid yourself—you most certainly are, then you can't make magic on demand.

Because you're not really the magician. Of course you're the one standing there on stage with a cape and wand, but don't think for a second you're the one who puts the rabbit in your hat for you to pull out.

Then how does the rabbit get there? I have my theories, but no finite proof as of yet. Maybe it's God. Maybe it's the collective, universal unconscious. Maybe it's angels, fairies, Martians, or martinis. All I know for sure is—it ain't you.

Don't believe me? Let's do an experiment. Go write a great sentence. I'll wait.

(posting a pic of a cute dog on Facebook)

Okay, you're back. Did you come to the words or did the words eventually come to you?

Really think about this for a moment.

In case you're not in the mood for this esoteric, semi-spiritual conversation, I'll just tell you what happened. The words came to you.

It's impossible to think your way to a great sentence.

In reality, you set your intention for a great sentence and then you have to wait for it to organize in your mind.

The sooner you accept this, the sooner your writing will come to life.

I promise.

A real writer must find the balancing point between action and surrender.

Is that the most critical piece of writing advice?

No.

That's next.

Maybe.

"The intellect has little to do on the road to discovery. There comes a leap in consciousness, call it intuition or what you will, and the solution comes to you and you don't know how or why."
—ALBERT EINSTEIN

CHAPTER 4

Have you been in love?

Although I hope it was mutual, I'm not asking if you've been loved back. I just need to know if you ever thoroughly loved. Even, or especially, a pet.

Good.

Beautiful.

We're on the same page. We both know what it feels like to be overwhelmed by a deep, uninhibited, and automatic knowing.

That's where you need to write from. And this, my dear friend, is the most critical piece of writing advice I can offer you.

Write from the place in your gut where love dwells.

The closer you get to this, the stronger the bond will become with your readers. It doesn't even matter if you are writing a physics textbook. Because, as you know, you can put two textbooks side by side, that cover the same material, and one will be readable, and the other will only be fit for kindling.

But let me warn you: it won't always feel like love. Writing, if you really care about it, can be an excruciating process. I've never given birth, but it must be in the same ballpark.

Once the pain and pushing is over, you'll feel the automatic, uninhibited love for your creation. Which is why you want to send your writing to everyone you know. You're proud of your new baby.

How do you write from the place in your gut where love dwells?

The Sufi poet Rumi said, "Your task is not to seek for love, but merely to seek and find all the barriers within yourself that you have built against it."

As you sit to write, sidestep all negativity like an Aikido master. Be brave. Allow yourself to keep your mind completely open in the balancing point between action and surrender.

And please remember, you're not the magician. You're an antenna. And you tune yourself in by getting out of your own way.

First, take a few deep breaths into your belly. No work of genius can come from shallow breathing.

Secondly, set your intention to receive and you will.

I promise you will.

Trust these two steps as you trust yourself when you're in love.

When you're in love, you can't be talked out of it. It's just something that simply exists.

Like gravity.

And like gravity, it won't be denied.

This is where you must write from. As if the universe depends on it.

Because it just might.

If you master this, you'll become one of the greats for sure.

"The writer must believe that what he is doing is the most important thing in the world. And he must hold to this illusion even when he knows it is not true."

—JOHN STEINBECK

CHAPTER 5

Repeat after me, "I, state your name, do hereby pledge, that under no circumstance will I dumb myself down."

Do not squander your gift with calculative attempts at appealing to the masses like one of those sycophantic, second-rate sitcoms.

You are here to be extraordinary, not ordinary.

Don't explain your jokes. Don't water down your wit. Don't make excuses for your knowledge. Don't tell half of the story because you're afraid people won't be able to get it.

If you remember to put yourself in the reader's shoes, if you resist rushing and if you write from your gut, they'll get it.

The Golden Rule applies here. Treat readers the way you want to be treated.

Do you want to be spoken to like a child? Of course not. But the general population is so accustomed to the patronizing manner in which they're handled, they think it's normal and natural. That's why you're going to separate yourself by assuming your audience is slick and a step or two above. Trust me, they'll love you for it.

Example:

I started this chapter with: I, state your name, do hereby pledge . . .

That's a subtle homage to *Animal House* and a nod to fans, like me, who know the movie by heart. Notice I didn't explain it away from the get-go, because if you picked up on it, you're going to feel like an insider. Like I speak your language. Now we're friends. Now you'll give a shit about me.

If movies aren't your thing, maybe you dug my usage of "sycophantic" or you liked that I put down bad TV.

Maybe I haven't won you over yet. At least you're still here so I must be doing something right.

"Everybody wants to feel that you're writing to a certain demographic because that's good business, but I've never done that . . . I tried to write stories that would interest me. I'd say, what would I like to read? . . . I don't think you can do your best work if you're writing for somebody else, because you never know what that somebody else really thinks or wants."

—STAN LEE

CHAPTER 6

I hate surfers.

They have perfectly defined bodies and I bet they never step foot in a gym or think twice about what they eat.

Alright, I don't hate them. Maybe I'm just jealous.

Okay, you got me. I'm totally jealous.

But what came first, the chicken or the egg?

Are these bastards driven to surf because they're born with Adonis attributes or did they get so goddamn good looking from surfing?

In other words, if I took up surfing, would I also end up looking like I'm ready for a *Men's Fitness* photo shoot?

I bring this up because I used the word "sycophants" in the last chapter and trust me, my vocabulary isn't that good. I heard that word in a Seal song many moons ago and I eventually got around to looking it up (a sycophant is an ass-kisser).

So, am I a writer because I was born with the proclivity to make note of everything or does my brain behave this way because I write?

Which one is it? I'm not sure. Probably both.

Since we can't know exactly, there's only one thing to do about it: write.

If you don't already pay attention to everything, start this moment. Squirrel away everything in your mind and you'll be amazed at what you can recall when a sentence calls for it.

There are legions of writers who popped out of their moms with much more talent than me, but I "made it" because I made myself make it. I didn't take no for an answer. When doors wouldn't open in the traditional manner, I kicked through them with brute force.

And I assure you, since you've brought yourself to these words, you have the Desire. And the Desire will bring you further than the most gifted writer who never picks up the pen.

In other words, you may never see me in *Men's Fitness*, but eventually, if I had the Desire, my boards would be waxed up and I'd be surfing.

Cowabonga, baby.

"You get ideas from daydreaming. You get ideas from being bored. You get ideas all the time. The only difference between writers and other people is we notice when we're doing it."

—NEIL GAIMAN

"We are told that talent creates its own opportunities. But it sometimes seems that intense desire creates not only its own opportunities, but its own talents."

—ERIC HOFFER

CHAPTER 7

"We conversed using the medium of instant messaging via our cellular telephones."

Maybe they speak this way at Mensa meetings, but no one I know uses lingo like this.

We took a pledge against dumbing ourselves down and now we must promise not to, umm, smarten ourselves up (obviously not a problem of mine).

"We texted." You're a real person. Your readers are real people. So keep it real.

There are times, however, when stuffy words are necessary. Take for example the Big Lebowski in *The Big Lebowski*. As it turns out, this character basically bloviates for a living so the writers of this movie were justified in having him spout out sentences like, "I just want to understand this, sir. Every time a rug is micturated upon in this fair city, I have to compensate the owner?"

Although you and I would have simply said, "Every time a rug is peed on . . ." it's appropriate for characters to stay true to themselves.

Please feel free to use a thesaurus but you'll be sniffed out as a phony in two seconds if it sounds like you relied on one. Bigger isn't always better. Remember, your goal as a writer is to connect with people. Forget about impressing anyone.

But I guarantee this: if you connect, they'll end up being impressed.

(I just read through this. I don't want you to think I'm against writing beautiful sentences because I certainly am not. But a beautiful sentence that doesn't connect with the reader is the same as an extravagantly ornate, plastic sword in a duel to the death. Useless.)

"Don't use words too big for the subject. Don't say 'infinitely' when you mean 'very'; otherwise you'll have no word left when you want to talk about something really infinite."

—C.S. LEWIS

CHAPTER 8

I'm sitting in a bookstore, staring at my iPad, and I've maybe typed eleven words in the last two hours.

I'm having dinner with my sister later and she just called to see if I'm getting anything accomplished. I said, "No, but I'm getting a lot of not-writing done."

Not-writing is just as important as writing. Maybe even more so.

It's the process of figuring out what not to put on paper.

For two days now, I've been wondering how to tell you about my writing style. And about fifteen minutes before my sister called, I finally realized why I've been having so much trouble and proceeded to delete a bunch of paragraphs (deleting is like throwing up your guts—it's painful but quite cathartic).

The seven words saved me: no one gives a shit about you.

I was rambling about my short sentences, short paragraphs and short chapters. But why talk about what's already obvious? I put myself in your shoes and said, "I don't give a rat's ass! Just tell me how this relates to me being a better writer!"

I'll get to that in the next chapter.

Serendipitously, not-writing entered the frame so we must give it its due coverage.

As writers, we want to see the page fill up with words, preferably, with brilliance and beauty. When it happens, we feel as if we've found a secret, peaceful path to the top of Everest. And when we're not-writing—figuring out what not to put on paper—we feel as if we're stuck in a storm, doing nothing at base camp. It feels unproductive. You can almost hear your life passing by.

Please remember to go easy on yourself here. Allow yourself to just sit and stare. You're not doing nothing. As you're waiting for the storm to pass, the Sherpas are surrounding your tent with Himalayan prayer flags. And I promise, those prayers will eventually be answered. So don't give up. And don't settle, under any circumstance, for a sentence that is less than your absolute best.

How can I be so sure about this? Because I've written over four hundred columns for *The Miami Herald* and was caught in the storm almost every time. But without fail, I conquered the mountain.

Don't second-guess yourself when something feels right, but don't rest until it does.

The delete key, the one in your mind and the one on your computer, is a valuable asset. Because at the end of the day, to quote myself from earlier, "I'd rather write ten words that will stir the souls of mankind than ten thousand that will never get past the flesh."

"What no wife of a writer can ever understand is that a writer is working when he's staring out of the window."

—BURTON RASCOE

CHAPTER 9

Lengthy paragraphs.

They're like daunting monoliths I'd rather not deal with.

When I see one approaching in a magazine or a book or even in an email, I'm like, "Jeez man, *really*?"

I have places to go, people to see, and unless your name is Hunter S. Thompson, I honestly don't even have the attention span to make it through what seems to be your seventy-sentence paragraph.

I keep my sentences, paragraphs, and chapters short because life is short. If you entrust me with your precious time, do you think I'd ever allow myself to waste it by wrestling around with you on the floor before actually saying something of value?

Even if you find the Holy Grail of sentences in the middle of a lengthy paragraph, it won't marinate in your mind as intended because the next sentence is already clamoring for your attention.

That's why I throw quick jabs. Not aimless ones into the wind, but jabs that land often and leave marks.

Shorten your paragraphs and leave the wrestling for the phonies.

"Not a wasted word. This has been a main point to my literary thinking all my life."

—HUNTER S. THOMPSON

CHAPTER 10

In his book *On Writing: A Memoir of the Craft,* Steven King says he writes with his wife in mind. If he manages to impress her, he knows he created a winner for his fans.

That made me think. Who do I trust more than anyone else? Who's the one person I should strive to impress?

Me.

I write with me in mind.

Because when it comes to writing, I'm not interested in good enough. Only perfection is permitted to prevail.

And it ain't easy. It's the antithesis of easy. I'm honestly intimidated every time I sit down in front of a blank screen. To me, writing is like putting together a five thousand piece puzzle. The pieces are no bigger than a quarter and you only have the faintest idea what the final picture is supposed to look like.

And if that's not uphill enough, half the time, you're blindfolded.

But when I sit down with the intention of nothing less than perfect, I eventually finish the puzzle. Not only do I always finish, it never fails to turn out more miraculous than I ever could have imagined.

As I read through what I've written, I thank the gods I wrote when I did because there's no way in hell I'd ever be able to do it as well again.

Should you keep someone in mind when you write?

If it improves your writing, most definitely.

Who should it be? Anyone who can be a catalyst to the miraculous.

"The most essential gift for a good writer is a built-in, shockproof shit detector. This is the writer's radar and all great writers have had it."

—ERNEST HEMINGWAY

"Easy reading is damn hard writing."

—NATHANIEL HAWTHORNE

CHAPTER 11

It was the best of sentences, it was the worst of sentences . . .

Your opening sentences critically need to be the best of sentences or I, no matter how much I dig you as a person, will turn my back on your second paragraph and leave it for the vultures.

I really don't even care if you carefully combined *The Catcher in the Rye* with *Star Wars*. It might be my loss, but if you don't intrigue me from the get-go, I'm gone with no regrets.

Literary agents and acquisition editors might be less brutal about this, but is it worth taking a chance?

It isn't.

You grant life to your opening lines for one purpose: to grab readers by their hearts, or if need be, their throats.

And once you have them, they'll beg you not to let go.

"Get comfortable because I want to tell you something.

Ready?

You're extraordinary."

"What really knocks me out is a book that, when you're all done reading it, you wish the author that wrote it was a terrific friend of yours and you could call him up on the phone whenever you felt like it. That doesn't happen much, though."

—J.D. SALINGER

CHAPTER 12

I'm at Starbucks watching an old man struggle with the zipper on his jacket. His hands are slightly shaking but he's keeping a smile. I'm dying to get up and help (and maybe even give him a hug), but I'm sure he'll eventually get it on his own.

Your characters need to be as real as this guy.

If they're trapped underwater, your readers should gasp for air. If they're chained to the bottom of the deep end of a pool, your readers should feel guilty for not being able to dive into your book with a pair of bolt cutters.

Overwhelming empathy is essential.

How do you write a character with an almost audible heartbeat?

You read the works of the authors you admire, you fearlessly forge your own style and write until there are blisters on your fingers.

In other words, you're on your own kid. You'll have to feel your way through.

My only advice for fiction writers is to figure out how to make your characters as real as the man who successfully zippered up his jacket and walked off into the sunset.

And of course, it would help to have a stellar story to tell.

"It is only when you open your veins and bleed onto the page a little that you establish contact with your reader. If you do not believe in the characters or the story you are doing at that moment with all your mind, strength, and will, if you don't feel joy and excitement while writing it, then you're wasting good white paper, even if it sells, because there are other ways in which a writer can bring in the rent money besides writing bad or phony stories."

—PAUL GALLICO

CHAPTER 13

Forget about your family and friends.

Not altogether of course, but you can forget about getting them on board. They just don't want you to try to become a writer.

The sooner you surrender to that, the sooner you'll be free of their expectations.

I'm sure they usually offer reliable advice, but you can't trust words of wisdom about living life outside of *The Matrix* from people who are thoroughly stuck inside of it.

What they don't understand is that you're not *trying* to become a writer. Because the thing is, we already *are* writers. What we're trying to do is "make it" in the world *as we are*.

"How will you keep up with the Joneses?"

Maybe we won't. But from my perspective, we've already eclipsed the Joneses because, unlike most others, we have the guts to follow our hearts.

So what should we do about all of this rejection from literary agents, publishers, *and* loved ones?

Keep writing. Keep writing and pay attention to how the universe unfolds.

"Writers will happen in the best of families."
—RITA MAE BROWN

CHAPTER 14

The Butterfly Effect

- As far back as I can remember, I wanted to be a writer. And what would I do about it? Nothing. Why bother if it's so difficult to get published? So I didn't write. Ever. All I did was complain about wanting to be a writer and gripe about my horrific corporate jobs.

- Annoyed with my constant bellyaching, a good friend told me I wasn't allowed to speak to her anymore until I started writing.

- So I started—crazy crap about girlfriends I've had and jobs I've been fired from. I had no idea where I was going with it, but it didn't matter. The butterfly flapped its wings.

- About two years later, I was having breakfast at a real hipster hangout in the Design District of Miami (I wasn't hip but my girlfriend at the time was). I saw a girl I went to college with at another table, but I avoided eye contact because I wasn't in the mood for small talk. It was out of my hands, however, because she approached me. Turns out she was writing professionally. I told her I dabbled in it a bit and she said, without giving me her email address, that I should email her some of my stuff. And then she walked away. I almost let her leave, but something in my gut moved me to follow her and ask for her card. She handed me an old ratty one.

- I really didn't want to email her because I basically had to beg for her card, but my gut told me to stay humble so I completed the circle and sent a chapter (I think it was about getting stuck in an elevator at one of my jobs. I had important documents the boss needed to quickly fax to the bank but there I was, caught in a sweltering elevator for thirty minutes).

- She emailed me back saying she loved it. This was a sign I was on the right path so I continued to deal with the rejection letters and kept writing.

- *The Miami Herald* called me a week later. The girl from the hipster hangout tipped them off about me. A week after that, my first column appeared in their newspaper.

- Years later, while still writing for *The Herald*, I started working on my book *Live Like a Fruit Fly*. I finished it in a year.

- I thought, since I wrote for a major newspaper, literary agents would chase after me like a pack of blood-famished zombies. Think again, Gabe. I was turned down by every literary agent I queried. Eventually I wrote letters to all of them. Twice.

- Screw it. I'll contact publishing houses directly. 100% rubber stamp rejected. Twice.

- Was I going to allow others to decide my destiny? Hells no. I self-published through a print-on-demand company and my book became available on amazon.com.

- Alan Colmes, a nationally syndicated talk show host, bought my book on amazon.com and loved it so much that he tracked me down and interviewed me on the air. Alan also asked me to write for his news site, where I'm still a contributor.

- Soon after, a friend of mine was looking at my book on amazon.com and her friend, who at the time was the acquisitions editor at HCI Books, was intrigued by the title.

- The contract was signed and HCI, the original publisher of the Chicken Soup for the Soul series, republished my book and it's now for sale in a store near you.

- Knowing Alan Colmes was friends with Deepak Chopra, one of the most respected spiritual authors of all time, I worked up the nerve to ask Alan to see if by some miracle, Deepak would read my book and then endorse it.

- One night while listening to his show, I heard Alan announce Deepak Chopra was going to be his next guest. Although I was nervous about it, this was a breadcrumb I had no choice but to follow. I sent Alan an email while he was on the air.

- "In *Live Like a Fruit Fly*, Gabe Berman shares his recipe for living a more joyful, worthwhile, and abundant life in every way. A witty, entertaining, and insightful read."
    —Deepak Chopra, Author, *The Seven Spiritual Laws of Success*

And the butterfly continues to flap its wings.

"The journey of a thousand miles begins with one step."

—LAO TZU

"Coincidence, if traced far enough back, becomes inevitable."

(NOT SURE WHO SAID THIS—ACCORDING TO THE INTERNET, MAYBE CARL JUNG OR MAYBE IT'S INSCRIBED ON A HINDU TEMPLE NEAR NEW DELHI. MAYBE BOTH.)

CHAPTER 15

"How do I start writing a book?"

I'm asked this question, and derivations of it, more than any other.

You have a great idea for a book, but you don't know how to write it.

Do you know why you don't know how to write a book?

Because nobody does. And that's why the idea of writing a book is so utterly overwhelming. There isn't a map. You're on your own.

But I've taken the journey to the top of the mountain and lived to tell about it. And although everything has worked out the way it had to, I'm going to share the secret I wish I knew years ago.

I hope you're ready.

Please grab a pen or pencil and a clean sheet of paper.

C'mon. I know you didn't do it.

How do I know? Because I wouldn't have either. But if you do, I promise you won't regret it. So pretty please, with sugar on top, go grab something to write with and get a clean sheet of paper.

Thank you.

In the center of the page, write down the following words in exactly this order and, if you can, please be neat about it:

> College level grammar
> Post graduate sentence structure
> Completed outline
> Constructed ending
> Character bios
> Central hypothesis
> List of literary agents
> List of publishers
> Marketing contacts
> Social media plan

Read the list over once.

Now fold it in half.

And finally, crumple it up and throw it in the garbage. By the time you master all of it, we could all be dead.

There's only one thing you must do to write a book: **Start it.**

You just sit down, buckle yourself in, and start writing.

That's it. That's the secret to greatness. That's the coveted path to mastery.

Everything else you spend time on is a diversionary tactic that will only keep you from your mission of writing the first sentence. The water isn't going to get any warmer than it already is. You must jump in. Now.

By the way, have you heard the latest about J.K. Rowling? She was kicked off the Forbes' billionaire list because she no longer qualified after giving $160 million to charity.

She started writing *Harry Potter* the same night the idea popped into her head. She was on welfare at the time.

So let me ask you, when are you going to start writing?

> *"A professional writer is an amateur who didn't quit."*
> —RICHARD BACH

– the end –